How to use this book

Follow the advice, in italics, given for you on each page.
Support the children as they read the text that is shaded in cream.
***Praise** the children at every step!*

Detailed guidance is provided in the Read Write Inc. Phonics Handbook

9 reading activities

Children:
Practise reading the speed sounds.
Read the green, red and challenge words for the story.
Listen as you read the introduction.
Discuss the vocabulary check with you.
Read the story.
Re-read the story and discuss the 'questions to talk about'.
Read the story with fluency and expression.
Answer the questions to 'read and answer'.
Practise reading the speed words.

Speed sounds

Consonants *Say the pure sounds (do not add 'uh').*

f ff	l ll le	m mm	n nn kn	r rr wr	s ss se	v ve	z zz s	sh	th	ng nk

b bb	c k ck	d dd	g gg	h	j	p pp	qu	t tt	w wh	x	y	ch tch

Vowels *Say the sounds in and out of order.*

at	hen head	in	on	up	day	see happy he	high find	blow no

zoo	look	car	for door snore	fair	whirl	shout	boy spoil

*Each box contains one sound but sometimes more than one grapheme. Focus graphemes are **circled**.*

Green words

Read in Fred Talk (pure sounds).

or horse tooth know most too seen grow north

whisk wrap chair pair air hair Blair

Read in syllables.

pill\`ow	→	pillow	chil\`dren	→	children
gor\`ill\`a	→	gorilla	tin\`sel	→	tinsel
pres\`ent	→	present	fair\`y	→	fairy
un\`fair	→	unfair	up\`stairs	→	upstairs
des\`pair	→	despair	hair\`dress\`er	→	hairdresser
mill\`i\`on\`aire	→	millionaire	post\`card	→	postcard

Read the root word first and then with the ending.

sparkle	→	sparkly	put	→	puts
wrap	→	wrapping	branch	→	branches
fairy	→	fairies	hair	→	hairy

Red words

could there

all they any

Challenge words

wand swaps Father Christmas

magic honest ball money

Hairy Fairy

Introduction

Would it be fair if you kept losing your job before you knew if you were any good at it or not? Is it right to have to change yourself just to fit in with other people?

This story is about a fairy.
He has a beautiful dress, a wand and wings just like other fairies but...there's a problem. He is covered in thick hair. Imagine what problems that gives him. No one will give him a job. But in the end he finds the perfect solution and he ends up better off than all the other fairies.

Find out how.

Story written by Gill Munton
Illustrated by Tim Archbold

Vocabulary check

Discuss the meaning (as used in the story) after the children have read each word.

	definition:	sentence/phrase:
frilly	*ruffled and lacy*	*a pink frilly dress*
fairy dust	*magic powder*	*a sack of fairy dust*
nips	*moves quickly*	*The tooth fairy nips into his bedroom.*
got the sack	*lost your job*	*So I got the sack.*
tinsel	*sparkly streamers*	*They put tinsel on the Christmas tree's branches.*
in an odd way	*strangely*	*He looked at me in an odd way.*
despair	*no ideas, no hope*	*The Fairy Queen looked at me in despair.*

Punctuation to note in this story:

1. Capital letters to start sentences and full stop to end sentences

2. Capital letters for names

3. Exclamation marks to show anger, shock and surprise

4. 'Wait and see' dots...

Hairy fairy

I'm a fairy. I am - honest!

I've got all the right things.

I've got a pink frilly dress ...

a pair of sparkly boots ...

a sack of fairy dust ...

a pair of gold wings ...

and a magic wand to whisk in the air.

But - and it's a big but - I'm hairy! Very hairy indeed.

It's just so unfair!

Well, you can have a hairy dog,
or a hairy horse,
or a hairy gorilla.

But a hairy fairy?
I don't think so!

Or I didn't think so,
until the Fairy Queen sent me to …

Let's begin at the beginning.

I started off as a tooth fairy.
You know – when a child has lost a tooth,
he puts it under his pillow at night.
The tooth fairy creeps upstairs,
nips into his bedroom,
and swaps the tooth for money.

It was a good job, that.
But the Fairy Queen said I might frighten
the children, so I got the sack.

I was a Christmas tree fairy next.

I was sent to live with Mr and Mrs Blair.

They got a big Christmas tree,

and put tinsel and glass balls on the branches.

They put fairy lights on, too.

And then they stuck me on the top.

But Mrs Blair said that a hairy fairy looked all wrong.

So that was the end of that.

Then the Fairy Queen sent me to the hairdresser.

He looked at me in an odd way

(hadn't he seen a hairy fairy before?),

but he started to snip.

I sat in that hairdresser's chair all day.

There was hair on the floor, hair in my lap,

hair on the chair ...

Things went all right for a week or so.

But then the hair started to grow back, thicker than before!

The Fairy Queen was in despair.
She didn't know what to do with me.

Then she had a postcard from Father Christmas.
He lives in the far north, as you know.
And he couldn't get any fairies to help him with the presents,
as most of them can't stand the snow and the frost.

But that's not a problem for a hairy fairy.
We hairy fairies don't feel the cold at all.

I spend my days wrapping presents,

and FC pays me very well for it.

In fact, I'm almost a millionaire!

Not bad, for a hairy fairy.

Questions to talk about

Re-read the page. Read the question to the children. Tell them whether it is a **FIND IT** *question or* **PROVE IT** *question.*

FIND IT

- ✓ *Turn to the page*
- ✓ *Read the question*
- ✓ *Find the answer*

PROVE IT

- ✓ *Turn to the page*
- ✓ *Read the question*
- ✓ *Find your evidence*
- ✓ *Explain why*

Page 9:	FIND IT	*What does the fairy wear?*
Page 10:	FIND IT	*Why does the hairy fairy think life isn't fair?*
Page 11:	FIND IT	*Why did the hairy fairy get the sack from the job of a tooth fairy?*
Page 12:	PROVE IT	*Do you think Mrs Blair should have kept the hairy fairy?*
Page 13:	PROVE IT	*How do you think the hairy fairy felt when his hair started to grow back?*
Page 14:	FIND IT	*Why is the hairy fairy a good person to work for Father Christmas?*
Page 15:	PROVE IT	*How does the hairy fairy feel about his hair in the end?*

Questions to read and answer

(Children complete without your help.)

1. The fairy had a **red spotty dress / a short black dress / a pink frilly dress.**

2. The tooth fairy swapped the tooth for **some sweets / money / a storybook.**

3. Mrs Blair said that a hairy fairy looked **fantastic / all wrong / very silly.**

4. The Fairy Queen sent him to **the hairdresser / the shops / the zoo.**

5. The hairy fairy is **very poor / very rich / very unhappy** at the end.

Speed words

Children practise reading the words across the rows, down the columns and in and out of order clearly and quickly.

children	before	tooth	horse	sparkly
too	hairy	fairy	upstairs	pair
unfair	chair	could	anything	most
don't	so	they	ball	very